PRINCEWILL LAGANG

Mastering Business: The Carlos Slim Success Blueprint

First published by PRINCEWILL LAGANG 2023

Copyright © 2023 by Princewill Lagang

All rights reserved. No part of this publication may be reproduced, stored or transmitted in any form or by any means, electronic, mechanical, photocopying, recording, scanning, or otherwise without written permission from the publisher. It is illegal to copy this book, post it to a website, or distribute it by any other means without permission.

Princewill Lagang asserts the moral right to be identified as the author of this work.

First edition

This book was professionally typeset on Reedsy. Find out more at reedsy.com

Contents

1. Seeds of Ambition — 1
2. Building the Empire: Strategic Investments and Innovations — 4
3. The Art of Adaptation: Navigating Economic Tides — 7
4. Legacy and Leadership Principles — 10
5. The Human Element: Relationships, Networks, and Social... — 13
6. Innovation, Disruption, and the Future Frontier — 16
7. Beyond Borders: Global Vision and Geopolitical Influence — 19
8. The Enduring Wisdom: Lessons for Future Generations — 22
9. A Glimpse into the Future: The Carlos Slim Legacy Unfolding — 25
10. The Evergreen Legacy: Enduring Principles for Success — 28
11. Continuity and Evolution: A Living Legacy — 31
12. The Legacy Continues: Nurturing Entrepreneurial Spirit — 34
13. Summary — 37

1

Seeds of Ambition

Title: Mastering Business: The Carlos Slim Success Blueprint

In the pulsating heart of Mexico City, where the vibrant energy of a bustling metropolis meets the echoes of history, a young Carlos Slim Helu embarked on a journey that would redefine the landscape of business. This chapter delves into the early life and formative experiences that sowed the seeds of ambition in the mind of a man who would later become one of the world's wealthiest and most influential entrepreneurs.

1.1 Origins in the Historic Tapestry

The narrative begins in the mid-20th century, a time when Mexico was undergoing profound social and economic changes. Against this backdrop, we explore Carlos Slim's familial roots, tracing his lineage and the values instilled in him by his Lebanese immigrant parents. The Helu family's journey, like many others, is interwoven with the threads of migration, hard work, and a relentless pursuit of the elusive Mexican Dream.

1.2 Shaping Young Minds: Early Education and Influences

Carlos Slim's childhood was marked by the confluence of traditional values and a rapidly evolving world. This section sheds light on his early education, exploring the impact of mentors and teachers who recognized and nurtured his exceptional intellect. From an early age, Slim displayed an insatiable curiosity and a penchant for numbers, foreshadowing the financial acumen that would later distinguish him in the business world.

1.3 The Rise of a Visionary: Formative Business Ventures

As a young man, Carlos Slim tested the waters of entrepreneurship with a series of small-scale business ventures. From buying shares in a Mexican bank to investing in real estate, these early experiences laid the groundwork for the strategic mindset that would define his future success. This section examines the risks taken, lessons learned, and the resilience displayed during the nascent stages of Slim's business career.

1.4 The Crucible of Adversity: Economic Downturn and Resilience

No success story is devoid of challenges, and Carlos Slim's journey is no exception. This part of the chapter explores how Slim navigated the stormy seas of economic downturns and financial crises. It investigates the pivotal moments that tested his resolve, revealing the resilience that allowed him to weather storms that would have deterred many.

1.5 Emergence of a Business Titan: Foundations of Grupo Carso

The chapter culminates in the formation of Grupo Carso, the conglomerate that would serve as the launchpad for Slim's meteoric rise. We dissect the strategic decisions, calculated risks, and the unique business philosophy that set Grupo Carso apart. This section sets the stage for the subsequent chapters, where we will delve into the intricacies of Slim's major business ventures and the principles that propelled him to the summit of global business success.

As we unravel the layers of Carlos Slim's early life and the genesis of his entrepreneurial spirit, readers are invited to glean insights from the experiences that molded a visionary business leader. The Carlos Slim Success Blueprint, as hinted at in this opening chapter, is a tapestry woven with determination, resilience, and an unwavering commitment to mastering the art of business.

2

Building the Empire: Strategic Investments and Innovations

Title: Mastering Business: The Carlos Slim Success Blueprint

2.1 Visionary Investments: Telecom and Beyond

With the foundations laid in the preceding chapter, we now delve into Carlos Slim's strategic investments that propelled him into the echelons of global business. The focal point is Slim's astute entry into the telecommunications industry, where he not only identified opportunities but also revolutionized the sector. This section dissects the calculated risks, market insights, and transformative vision that led to the creation of Telmex, marking the beginning of Slim's ascent to business magnate status.

2.2 The Art of Monopoly: Telmex and America Movil Dominance

As Slim's telecommunications empire expanded, so did the scrutiny surrounding his business practices. This part of the chapter examines the challenges and controversies that arose as Telmex and America Movil became dominant players not only in Mexico but across Latin America. We explore the art of maintaining market leadership, the complexities of competition, and the criticisms faced by Slim as he navigated through uncharted territory.

2.3 Diversification Strategies: Grupo Carso's Multifaceted Approach

Beyond telecommunications, Carlos Slim demonstrated a penchant for diversification. This section delves into Grupo Carso's expansion into various industries, including retail, construction, and healthcare. The chapter explores the synergies created by Slim's diverse portfolio, showcasing his ability to identify emerging markets and capitalize on strategic opportunities.

2.4 The Philanthropic Arm: The Carlos Slim Foundation

Embedded within the narrative of entrepreneurial success is Slim's commitment to philanthropy. This part of the chapter unveils the establishment and evolution of the Carlos Slim Foundation. We analyze the philanthropic initiatives that have left an indelible mark on education, healthcare, and social development, shedding light on Slim's belief in using wealth for the betterment of society.

2.5 Lessons from the Boardroom: Leadership and Management Philosophy

As the business empire expanded, so did the challenges of leadership. This section explores Carlos Slim's unique leadership style and management philosophy. Drawing from his experiences in steering Grupo Carso through economic fluctuations and industry disruptions, we extract lessons in resilience, adaptability, and long-term vision that entrepreneurs can apply to their own ventures.

2.6 Innovations and Future Trends: The Carlos Slim Approach

The chapter concludes by examining Slim's approach to innovation and his foresight in anticipating future trends. From embracing technology to adapting to changing consumer behaviors, this section provides insights into how Slim positioned his businesses for long-term success in an ever-evolving global landscape.

As we navigate through the strategic investments, controversies, diversification, philanthropy, and leadership insights of Carlos Slim, readers are invited to draw inspiration from a man whose mastery of business extends beyond financial success to leaving a lasting impact on the industries he touched and the communities he served. The Carlos Slim Success Blueprint unfolds as a dynamic playbook, showcasing the intersection of vision, resilience, and innovation in the world of business.

3

The Art of Adaptation: Navigating Economic Tides

Title: Mastering Business: The Carlos Slim Success Blueprint

3.1 Economic Tides and Global Shifts

Carlos Slim's journey through the business world has been shaped not only by his strategic brilliance but also by his ability to navigate the complex currents of global economics. This chapter delves into how Slim's businesses weathered economic storms, examining his responses to recessions, currency crises, and other macroeconomic challenges. From the Latin American debt crisis to the dot-com bubble, we explore the art of adaptation that allowed Slim to not only survive but thrive in changing economic landscapes.

3.2 Financial Engineering: The Slim Approach to Crisis Management

At the heart of Slim's success lies a mastery of financial engineering. This section analyzes how Slim utilized innovative financial strategies to navigate through turbulent times. From debt restructuring to strategic mergers and acquisitions, readers gain insights into the financial acumen that enabled Slim to turn challenges into opportunities and position his businesses for sustained growth.

3.3 Globalization and International Expansion

As markets became increasingly interconnected, Carlos Slim recognized the importance of globalization. This part of the chapter examines Slim's foray into international markets, exploring the challenges and triumphs of expanding his business empire beyond the borders of Mexico. From negotiations with international partners to the cultural nuances of operating in diverse regions, readers gain a comprehensive understanding of Slim's global business strategies.

3.4 Technology and Digital Transformation

In the 21st century, the rapid pace of technological advancement brought both challenges and opportunities. This section explores how Carlos Slim embraced digital transformation, from investing in technology companies to adapting traditional business models. Readers witness the evolution of Grupo Carso in the digital age and the lessons that emerge from Slim's ability to harness the power of innovation.

3.5 Sustainable Business Practices

A key element of Carlos Slim's business philosophy is a commitment to sustainability. This part of the chapter delves into Slim's initiatives to integrate environmental and social responsibility into business practices. From sustainable development projects to eco-friendly business ventures, readers gain insights into how Slim approached the intersection of profitability and social impact.

3.6 Legacy and Future Challenges

The chapter concludes by examining Carlos Slim's legacy and the challenges that lie ahead. From succession planning within Grupo Carso to the ongoing evolution of industries, readers are invited to contemplate the enduring principles embedded in the Carlos Slim Success Blueprint. As we reflect on Slim's journey through economic tides, the chapter sets the stage for the final section, where we explore the broader implications of his business philosophy for entrepreneurs and business leaders worldwide.

In traversing the economic landscapes that shaped Carlos Slim's journey, readers gain a nuanced understanding of the art of adaptation—a crucial element of the Carlos Slim Success Blueprint. The ability to navigate economic tides with resilience, strategic thinking, and a commitment to sustainable practices emerges as a hallmark of Slim's enduring influence in the world of business.

4

Legacy and Leadership Principles

Title: Mastering Business: The Carlos Slim Success Blueprint

4.1 The Architect of Legacy: Building for Generations

Carlos Slim's impact extends far beyond the realms of business. In this chapter, we explore the notion of legacy as a guiding force in Slim's entrepreneurial journey. From the creation of enduring institutions within Grupo Carso to his investments in education and cultural endeavors, readers gain insights into Slim's deliberate efforts to leave a lasting imprint on the world.

4.2 Succession Planning: Passing the Torch

As a business titan, one of Slim's pivotal challenges was ensuring the continuity of his legacy. This section delves into the intricacies of succession planning within Grupo Carso. From grooming the next generation of leaders to balancing family and professional dynamics, readers gain a front-row seat to the meticulous process of passing the torch and preserving the essence of Slim's entrepreneurial spirit.

4.3 Leadership Principles: A Playbook for Success

At the core of Carlos Slim's success is a set of principles that have shaped his leadership philosophy. This part of the chapter distills key leadership lessons drawn from Slim's experiences. From fostering innovation and adaptability to cultivating a culture of integrity and social responsibility, readers uncover a playbook for success that transcends industries and resonates with aspiring entrepreneurs and seasoned leaders alike.

4.4 Ethical Business Practices: The Moral Compass

Slim's success is not only measured in financial terms but also in the ethical framework that underpins his business practices. This section explores the moral compass that has guided Slim through complex decisions, ethical dilemmas, and the responsibilities that come with immense wealth. From corporate governance to transparency, readers gain insights into the ethical considerations that define the Carlos Slim Success Blueprint.

4.5 Mentorship and Learning: Wisdom Transcending Generations

Carlos Slim's journey is marked by the mentorship he received and, in turn, the mentorship he provided. This part of the chapter examines Slim's role as a mentor, both within his family and in the broader business community. Readers witness how the exchange of wisdom and the cultivation of a learning culture have been integral to Slim's leadership style, fostering a legacy that transcends generations.

4.6 Challenges and Opportunities for Future Leaders

The chapter concludes by examining the challenges and opportunities awaiting future leaders who seek to follow in the footsteps of Carlos Slim. From the impact of technological disruptions to the imperative of sustainable business practices, readers are prompted to consider the evolving landscape of business and the enduring relevance of the principles embedded in the Carlos Slim Success Blueprint.

As we explore the legacy, leadership principles, and ethical considerations that define Carlos Slim's impact on the business world, readers are invited to reflect on their own leadership journey. The Carlos Slim Success Blueprint emerges not just as a roadmap to financial success but as a guide to building a meaningful legacy, fostering ethical practices, and shaping the next generation of visionary leaders.

5

The Human Element: Relationships, Networks, and Social Capital

Title: Mastering Business: The Carlos Slim Success Blueprint

5.1 The Power of Connections: Building Networks

Carlos Slim's success is not only attributed to financial acumen but also to his ability to cultivate meaningful relationships. This chapter delves into the importance of networks in Slim's journey. From early collaborations to strategic partnerships, readers gain insights into how Slim leveraged social capital to open doors, create opportunities, and navigate the intricate web of business relationships.

5.2 Negotiation Mastery: Art and Science

At the heart of Slim's success lies his prowess in negotiation. This section explores the art and science of negotiation that has been instrumental in his business triumphs. From landmark deals to diplomatic collaborations, readers witness Slim's strategic approach to bargaining, compromise, and the delicate balance of power in the ever-evolving landscape of global business.

5.3 Corporate Citizenship: Social Responsibility in Action

Carlos Slim's impact extends beyond the boardroom, encompassing a commitment to corporate citizenship. This part of the chapter delves into Slim's philanthropic endeavors and the ways in which he has used his influence and resources to address social challenges. From community development projects to initiatives promoting education and healthcare, readers gain insights into the transformative power of corporate social responsibility within the Carlos Slim Success Blueprint.

5.4 Entrepreneurial Ecosystems: Fostering Innovation and Collaboration

Slim's journey reflects a deep understanding of the importance of fostering entrepreneurial ecosystems. This section explores how he contributed to the development of environments that nurture innovation and collaboration. From supporting startups to investing in research and development, readers gain a comprehensive view of Slim's role in shaping ecosystems that go beyond individual businesses, contributing to the broader tapestry of economic growth.

5.5 Crisis Management through Relationships: Lessons in Resilience

In times of crisis, the strength of relationships becomes paramount. This part of the chapter examines how Carlos Slim navigated through challenging periods by relying on his networks. From financial downturns to industry-specific challenges, readers gain insights into the role of relationships as a pillar of resilience and an asset in crisis management.

5.6 Looking Forward: The Social Capital Imperative

The chapter concludes by exploring the future of social capital in the business landscape. As technology redefines the way we connect and collaborate, readers are prompted to consider the evolving dynamics of relationships and the enduring importance of the human element in business success. The Carlos Slim Success Blueprint, as illuminated through the lens of social capital, serves as a testament to the transformative power of connections and the ripple effects of positive relationships.

As we navigate through the intricacies of networks, negotiations, and social responsibility in Carlos Slim's journey, readers are invited to contemplate their own approach to relationships in the business world. The Carlos Slim Success Blueprint emerges not just as a financial strategy but as a holistic guide that recognizes the profound impact of human connections on the trajectory of success in business and beyond.

6

Innovation, Disruption, and the Future Frontier

Title: Mastering Business: The Carlos Slim Success Blueprint

6.1 The Innovation Imperative: Pioneering Industry Trends

Carlos Slim's journey is marked by a keen sense of innovation that goes beyond adapting to current trends. This chapter explores how Slim has been a trailblazer, pioneering industry trends and staying ahead of the curve. From technological advancements to business model innovations, readers gain insights into Slim's mindset as an innovator and how he strategically positioned his businesses to thrive in a rapidly evolving business landscape.

6.2 Technology as a Catalyst: Digital Transformation Across Industries

The 21st century witnessed an unprecedented wave of technological disruption. This section delves into how Carlos Slim harnessed the power of technology to transform not only his telecommunications empire but also various industries within Grupo Carso. From e-commerce ventures to digital services, readers witness Slim's strategic embrace of technology as a catalyst for business growth and market leadership.

6.3 Risk-Taking and Experimentation: Lessons from Failure

Innovation often comes with inherent risks, and Slim's journey is no exception. This part of the chapter explores instances where Slim took calculated risks, experimented with new ventures, and faced failures. Readers gain insights into the resilience and adaptability required to navigate the uncertainties of innovation, shedding light on the lessons drawn from setbacks and the role of failure in the path to success.

6.4 Sustainability and Green Innovation: Navigating the Environmental Frontier

As the world grapples with environmental challenges, this section examines Carlos Slim's commitment to sustainability and green innovation. From eco-friendly business practices to investments in renewable energy, readers gain a comprehensive view of Slim's approach to balancing business growth with environmental stewardship. The chapter explores how sustainability has become a cornerstone of the Carlos Slim Success Blueprint in the face of a changing global landscape.

6.5 Disruption in Legacy Industries: The Art of Reinvention

Legacy industries are not immune to the winds of change, and Slim's businesses are a testament to the art of reinvention. This part of the chapter explores how Slim navigated disruption in traditional sectors, such as retail and construction. From adapting business models to embracing new technologies, readers gain insights into the strategic decisions that allowed Slim to stay relevant and maintain market leadership.

6.6 The Future Frontier: Artificial Intelligence, Biotech, and Beyond

The chapter concludes by peering into the future frontier of business and innovation. From artificial intelligence to biotechnology, readers are invited to contemplate the potential impact of emerging technologies on the business landscape. The Carlos Slim Success Blueprint, as seen through the lens of innovation, serves as a guide for navigating uncharted territories and staying at the forefront of industries yet to come.

As we explore the realms of innovation, disruption, and the future frontier, readers are prompted to reflect on their own approach to embracing change and staying ahead in a dynamic business environment. The Carlos Slim Success Blueprint emerges as a living document that not only captures the essence of past achievements but also serves as a compass for navigating the uncharted waters of innovation in the ever-evolving landscape of business.

7

Beyond Borders: Global Vision and Geopolitical Influence

Title: Mastering Business: The Carlos Slim Success Blueprint

7.1 Visionary Global Expansion: From Local Mogul to International Player

Carlos Slim's journey is not confined to the borders of Mexico; it extends across continents, reflecting a visionary global perspective. This chapter explores Slim's strategic foray into international markets, the challenges encountered, and the lessons learned. From cultural adaptations to geopolitical considerations, readers gain insights into the nuances of expanding a business empire beyond national boundaries.

7.2 Diplomacy and Business: Navigating Geopolitical Realities

As an influential figure in the business world, Carlos Slim's journey intersects with geopolitical landscapes. This section delves into how Slim navigated the complexities of international relations, political changes, and diplomatic considerations. From collaborations with foreign governments to managing business interests in regions with diverse political climates, readers gain a deeper understanding of the intersection between business success and geopolitical realities.

7.3 Global Economic Trends: Anticipating and Adapting

Success in the global arena requires a keen awareness of economic trends on a global scale. This part of the chapter explores how Carlos Slim anticipated and adapted to major global economic shifts. From the impact of financial crises to the opportunities presented by emerging markets, readers gain insights into the macroeconomic considerations that shaped Slim's global business strategies.

7.4 Cultural Intelligence: Navigating Diversity in Business Practices

Cultural intelligence is a critical asset for any global business leader. This section examines how Carlos Slim honed his cultural intelligence, understanding and navigating diverse business practices, social norms, and consumer behaviors across different regions. From managing multicultural teams to tailoring business approaches to local contexts, readers gain valuable insights into the importance of cultural sensitivity in global business endeavors.

7.5 Challenges and Triumphs: Lessons from Global Ventures

Success on the global stage is often accompanied by a unique set of challenges. This part of the chapter explores the trials and triumphs of Carlos Slim's global ventures. From regulatory hurdles to competition with local players, readers gain a comprehensive view of the obstacles faced and the strategic maneuvers employed to secure success in diverse international markets.

7.6 The Global Citizen: Philanthropy and Social Impact on a Global Scale

Carlos Slim's influence extends beyond business to the realm of global citizenship. This section examines Slim's philanthropic initiatives on an international scale, addressing global challenges such as healthcare, education, and poverty. Readers witness how the Carlos Slim Success Blueprint transcends national borders, contributing to positive social impact on a global scale.

As we explore the global dimensions of Carlos Slim's business empire, readers are invited to reflect on the interconnectedness of business, geopolitics, and global citizenship. The Carlos Slim Success Blueprint emerges as a testament to the transformative power of a global vision, strategic adaptability, and a commitment to making a positive impact on a worldwide scale.

8

The Enduring Wisdom: Lessons for Future Generations

Title: Mastering Business: The Carlos Slim Success Blueprint

8.1 Reflections on a Journey: Wisdom Gleaned from Experience

As we approach the culmination of this exploration into the Carlos Slim Success Blueprint, this chapter invites readers to reflect on the journey thus far. Drawing from the wealth of experiences and insights gleaned from Slim's life, this section sets the stage for distilling the enduring wisdom that transcends the specifics of industries, economies, and eras.

8.2 The Power of Long-Term Vision: Beyond Immediate Gains

At the core of Carlos Slim's success is a commitment to long-term vision. This part of the chapter delves into the wisdom of looking beyond immediate gains and navigating business with a perspective that extends far into the future. Readers are encouraged to contemplate the importance of patience, strategic foresight, and the discipline required to build lasting success over time.

8.3 Balancing Innovation and Tradition: A Dynamic Equation

The Carlos Slim Success Blueprint is characterized by a delicate balance between innovation and tradition. This section explores how Slim's journey reflects an ability to embrace new ideas and technologies while respecting the foundations of established industries. Readers are prompted to consider the dynamic equation of balancing innovation and tradition in their own entrepreneurial pursuits.

8.4 The Holistic Approach: Integrating Business and Philanthropy

A key pillar of Carlos Slim's legacy is the integration of business success with a commitment to philanthropy. This part of the chapter examines the wisdom behind this holistic approach, emphasizing the positive impact that businesses can have on society. Readers are invited to explore how their own endeavors can contribute to the betterment of communities and the world at large.

8.5 Leadership as a Force for Good: Ethics and Responsibility

The Carlos Slim Success Blueprint places a strong emphasis on ethical leadership and social responsibility. This section explores the wisdom behind leading with integrity, transparency, and a sense of responsibility to stakeholders. Readers are encouraged to reflect on how ethical leadership can not only drive business success but also contribute to the greater good.

8.6 Continual Learning and Adaptation: Keys to Sustained Relevance

As we approach the conclusion of the blueprint, the chapter emphasizes the importance of continual learning and adaptation. Carlos Slim's journey is marked by a commitment to staying informed, adapting to changing circumstances, and embracing new opportunities. Readers are prompted to cultivate a mindset of lifelong learning and agility to navigate the ever-evolving landscape of business.

8.7 The Ever-Evolving Blueprint: A Call to Action

The chapter concludes by acknowledging that the Carlos Slim Success Blueprint is not a static document but an ever-evolving guide. As readers embark on their own entrepreneurial journeys, they are challenged to contribute to the ongoing evolution of this blueprint. The call to action is clear: to draw inspiration from the wisdom imparted, apply these lessons in diverse contexts, and continue shaping the blueprint for success in an ever-changing world.

In this final chapter, readers are invited to internalize the wisdom distilled from Carlos Slim's journey and apply it to their own endeavors. The Carlos Slim Success Blueprint stands not as a final destination but as a dynamic and living guide, offering timeless principles that can inspire and guide future generations of entrepreneurs and business leaders.

9

A Glimpse into the Future: The Carlos Slim Legacy Unfolding

Title: Mastering Business: The Carlos Slim Success Blueprint

9.1 Legacy in Motion: The Next Chapter

As we turn the page to envision the future, this chapter serves as a glimpse into the unfolding legacy of Carlos Slim. It explores the ongoing impact of his endeavors, examining how the principles of the Carlos Slim Success Blueprint continue to shape businesses, communities, and global initiatives. Readers are invited to witness the dynamic legacy in motion, adapting to contemporary challenges and opportunities.

9.2 Evolution of Grupo Carso: Adapting to Changing Markets

This section delves into the evolution of Grupo Carso in the post-Carlos Slim era. It explores how the conglomerate has navigated changing markets, embraced new technologies, and maintained its position as a driver of economic growth. Readers gain insights into how Grupo Carso continues to uphold the values and principles instilled by Slim while adapting to the demands of a rapidly evolving business landscape.

9.3 The Next Generation: Carrying the Torch

A crucial aspect of any enduring legacy is the role of the next generation. This part of the chapter examines how the heirs of Carlos Slim have taken up the mantle, contributing their perspectives, innovations, and leadership to sustain and build upon the family legacy. Readers witness the interplay between tradition and innovation as the next generation carries the torch forward.

9.4 Impact on Social and Environmental Fronts: A Continued Commitment

The Carlos Slim Success Blueprint is inseparable from its commitment to social and environmental causes. This section explores how the legacy extends beyond business, detailing the ongoing impact of philanthropic initiatives and sustainable practices. Readers gain a deeper understanding of how the Carlos Slim legacy continues to contribute to positive change on a global scale.

9.5 Global Influence: Shaping Geopolitics and Diplomacy

The chapter also examines the enduring global influence of Carlos Slim. Whether through diplomatic endeavors, international collaborations, or contributions to global economic discussions, readers witness the ongoing impact of Slim's legacy on geopolitics. The chapter prompts readers to contemplate how individual business success can transcend borders and contribute to shaping a more interconnected world.

9.6 Lessons for Future Generations: A Blueprint for Tomorrow

As we peer into the future, this section distills key lessons from the Carlos

Slim Success Blueprint for the entrepreneurs and leaders of tomorrow. It serves as a guide for navigating the uncertainties of a rapidly changing world, emphasizing the timeless principles that have stood the test of time. Readers are encouraged to draw inspiration from the blueprint as they chart their own courses toward success and impact.

9.7 Epilogue: The Everlasting Impact

The chapter concludes with an epilogue that reflects on the everlasting impact of Carlos Slim's journey. It contemplates the enduring legacy that extends beyond individual achievements to shape industries, inspire leaders, and contribute to the betterment of society. The epilogue serves as a tribute to a business luminary whose influence echoes through the corridors of time.

In this final chapter, readers are invited to envision the unfolding legacy of Carlos Slim and contemplate their own roles in shaping the future of business and society. The Carlos Slim Success Blueprint, as it continues to evolve, stands as a testament to the transformative power of visionary leadership, strategic acumen, and a commitment to making a positive impact that resonates across generations.

10

The Evergreen Legacy: Enduring Principles for Success

Title: Mastering Business: The Carlos Slim Success Blueprint

10.1 The Enduring Principles: A Recapitulation

As we arrive at the final chapter, this section serves as a recapitulation of the enduring principles that constitute the Carlos Slim Success Blueprint. It revisits the key themes and lessons woven throughout the journey, reinforcing the foundational pillars that have guided Carlos Slim and continue to serve as beacons for aspiring entrepreneurs and business leaders.

10.2 Wisdom Beyond Borders: A Global Relevance

The wisdom embedded in the Carlos Slim Success Blueprint transcends borders and cultures. This part of the chapter explores how the principles elucidated in the blueprint possess a global relevance, offering insights and guidance to business leaders navigating diverse economic, political, and social landscapes. Readers are encouraged to embrace the universality of these principles in their own entrepreneurial endeavors.

10.3 The Blueprint in Practice: Case Studies and Examples

This section brings the Carlos Slim Success Blueprint to life through practical case studies and examples. It examines how entrepreneurs and businesses across different industries have applied Slim's principles to achieve success, overcome challenges, and contribute positively to their communities. These real-world illustrations serve as inspiration and practical guides for readers seeking to implement the blueprint in their own ventures.

10.4 Challenges and Opportunities in a New Era

As we contemplate the future, this part of the chapter addresses the challenges and opportunities that may arise in a new era of business. From technological advancements to shifts in consumer behavior, readers are prompted to consider how the Carlos Slim Success Blueprint can be adapted and applied to navigate the ever-changing landscape of the business world.

10.5 Mentorship and Passing the Torch: A Call to Action

The blueprint is not only a guide for individual success but also a call to action for mentorship and knowledge sharing. This section explores the importance of passing the torch to the next generation of entrepreneurs and business leaders. It encourages seasoned professionals to share their experiences, insights, and wisdom, contributing to the cultivation of a community that thrives on the principles outlined in the Carlos Slim Success Blueprint.

10.6 Epitome of Mastering Business: A Legacy Unparalleled

The chapter culminates in an exploration of how the Carlos Slim Success Blueprint stands as an epitome of mastering business. It reflects on the unparalleled legacy that Carlos Slim has left in the business world—a legacy defined not only by financial success but by the enduring impact on industries, communities, and the very fabric of global commerce.

10.7 Final Thoughts: The Evergreen Wisdom

In the final thoughts of the chapter, readers are left with reflections on the evergreen wisdom encapsulated in the Carlos Slim Success Blueprint. The journey may have concluded, but the blueprint lives on, offering a timeless guide for those who aspire to master the art of business, leave a lasting legacy, and contribute to the continual evolution of the global business landscape.

In closing, this chapter invites readers to carry the torch of the Carlos Slim Success Blueprint into the future, embodying its principles, and contributing to the ongoing narrative of success, innovation, and positive impact in the world of business.

11

Continuity and Evolution: A Living Legacy

Title: Mastering Business: The Carlos Slim Success Blueprint

11.1 The Living Legacy: Unfolding Chapters

This chapter unfolds as a continuation of the Carlos Slim Success Blueprint, exploring the dynamic nature of the legacy left by Carlos Slim. It delves into how the principles and philosophies elucidated throughout this narrative are not static but evolve in response to an ever-changing business landscape. Readers are invited to witness the unfolding chapters of this living legacy.

11.2 Adapting to New Realities: Lessons from Contemporary Challenges

As the business world faces new challenges and opportunities, this section explores how the Carlos Slim Success Blueprint adapts to contemporary realities. From the impact of global events to technological advancements, readers gain insights into how the blueprint continues to provide valuable guidance in navigating the complexities of the modern business environment.

11.3 Innovations in Leadership: The Next Generation's Influence

The chapter examines how the principles of leadership and business innovation, integral to the Carlos Slim Success Blueprint, are evolving with the influence of the next generation. It explores how emerging leaders are infusing new perspectives, technologies, and ideologies into the blueprint, ensuring its relevance in an era marked by rapid advancements and paradigm shifts.

11.4 Philanthropy and Social Impact: Expanding Horizons

The commitment to philanthropy and social impact, central to the Carlos Slim Success Blueprint, continues to expand its horizons. This section delves into how contemporary challenges, such as global health crises and environmental concerns, shape the philanthropic initiatives aligned with the blueprint. Readers witness the blueprint's ongoing contribution to addressing pressing societal issues.

11.5 Global Collaboration: The Blueprint in a Connected World

In an era of increased global connectivity, this part of the chapter explores how the Carlos Slim Success Blueprint fosters global collaboration. It examines how businesses and entrepreneurs, inspired by the blueprint, collaborate across borders, share knowledge, and collectively address challenges on a scale previously unimaginable.

11.6 The Blueprint in Education: Shaping Future Leaders

Education is a cornerstone of the blueprint's enduring influence. This section delves into how the principles outlined in the Carlos Slim Success Blueprint are integrated into educational curricula, shaping the minds of future leaders.

Readers witness the blueprint's impact on cultivating a new generation of business professionals equipped with the wisdom to navigate complexities.

11.7 Looking Ahead: A Blueprint for Generations to Come

The chapter concludes by looking ahead to the future chapters of the Carlos Slim Success Blueprint. It prompts readers to contemplate their role in the continued evolution of the blueprint, ensuring its resonance for generations to come. As the legacy of Carlos Slim unfolds, the blueprint remains a guiding force for those aspiring to master the intricacies of business in an ever-evolving world.

In this final chapter, readers are encouraged to see the Carlos Slim Success Blueprint not as a concluded narrative but as an ongoing story—an evolving guide that continues to shape the world of business, leadership, and philanthropy. As readers contribute their own chapters to this living legacy, the blueprint remains a source of inspiration, wisdom, and timeless principles for the dynamic journey of mastering business.

12

The Legacy Continues: Nurturing Entrepreneurial Spirit

Title: Mastering Business: The Carlos Slim Success Blueprint

12.1 A Legacy of Inspiration: Nurturing Entrepreneurial Aspirations

This final chapter reflects on the enduring legacy of Carlos Slim, focusing on the continued inspiration his journey provides to aspiring entrepreneurs. It explores how the blueprint serves as a source of motivation, empowering individuals to pursue their entrepreneurial aspirations with resilience, vision, and a commitment to making a positive impact.

12.2 Entrepreneurship in the Modern Era: New Frontiers and Challenges

As the blueprint influences contemporary entrepreneurship, this section delves into the dynamics of the modern business landscape. It explores new frontiers and challenges faced by entrepreneurs, emphasizing how the timeless principles embedded in the Carlos Slim Success Blueprint remain relevant in navigating the complexities of the ever-evolving business environment.

12.3 Innovation and Disruption: Adapting to a Rapidly Changing World

In a world characterized by rapid innovation and disruption, the chapter explores how the blueprint guides entrepreneurs in adapting to change. It examines the principles of innovation, agility, and strategic thinking, providing insights into how entrepreneurs can thrive amid technological advancements and shifts in consumer behavior.

12.4 Sustainable Entrepreneurship: A Blueprint for a Better Future

Sustainability is a key consideration in contemporary business practices. This section explores how the Carlos Slim Success Blueprint contributes to the rise of sustainable entrepreneurship. It examines how entrepreneurs can integrate environmental and social responsibility into their ventures, aligning with the blueprint's commitment to creating a positive impact on both business and society.

12.5 Collaboration and Networking: Building a Global Community

The chapter underscores the importance of collaboration and networking in the entrepreneurial journey. It explores how the blueprint fosters the creation of a global community, where entrepreneurs connect, share insights, and collaborate across borders. Readers are encouraged to leverage the blueprint as a tool for building meaningful relationships and expanding their entrepreneurial networks.

12.6 The Human Element: Values, Ethics, and Leadership

At the heart of the Carlos Slim Success Blueprint is a focus on the human element in business. This section delves into the enduring values, ethics, and leadership principles that guide entrepreneurs in building not only successful enterprises but also ethical and responsible organizations. It highlights the blueprint's emphasis on creating businesses that contribute positively to the well-being of individuals and communities.

12.7 Passing the Torch: Mentoring Future Leaders

The chapter concludes with a call to action for established entrepreneurs and business leaders to pass the torch of knowledge and mentorship. It explores how the blueprint's principles can be shared and imparted to the next generation, ensuring a legacy of wisdom and guidance that continues to shape the trajectory of entrepreneurial success.

In this final chapter, readers are invited to reflect on their own entrepreneurial journeys, drawing inspiration from the enduring legacy of Carlos Slim. As the blueprint continues to influence and nurture entrepreneurial spirit, it remains a guiding force for those who seek to master the complexities of business, leaving a positive imprint on the world and inspiring future generations of entrepreneurs.

13

Summary

Mastering Business: The Carlos Slim Success Blueprint is a comprehensive exploration of the life, principles, and impact of one of the most successful entrepreneurs of our time. The narrative spans twelve chapters, each unveiling a different facet of Carlos Slim's journey and distilling valuable lessons for aspiring business leaders.

The blueprint begins by delving into Slim's early life and the formative experiences that shaped his entrepreneurial spirit. It progresses through chapters that dissect the key elements of his success, including strategic business acumen, adaptability to economic shifts, mastery of financial engineering, globalization, and a commitment to sustainability.

Chapters unfold to explore Slim's legacy, succession planning, leadership principles, ethical business practices, and the importance of mentorship. The narrative navigates through Slim's approach to relationships, negotiations, corporate citizenship, and the management of crises, providing readers with a holistic view of the principles that underpin his success.

As the blueprint progresses, it adapts to the contemporary business landscape, exploring topics such as innovation, technology, disruption, and the ever-important human element in business. The narrative considers Slim's impact on a global scale, examining his diplomatic endeavors and the intersection of business with geopolitics.

The later chapters peer into the future, contemplating the ongoing legacy of Carlos Slim, the evolution of his business empire, and the challenges and opportunities that lie ahead. The blueprint emphasizes the importance of continuity, adaptation, and the passing of knowledge to future generations.

Ultimately, the Carlos Slim Success Blueprint is not a static document but a living guide. It transcends borders, industries, and eras, offering timeless principles for mastering the intricacies of business. It inspires aspiring entrepreneurs to embrace innovation, sustainability, ethical leadership, and the human element in their pursuits. As the blueprint evolves, it continues to shape the narrative of success, contributing to a global community of entrepreneurs committed to making a positive impact on the world.

www.ingramcontent.com/pod-product-compliance
Lightning Source LLC
LaVergne TN
LVHW020456080526
838202LV00057B/5977